Taking care of your
DOG

A Young Pet Owner's Guide
by Helen Piers

Consulting Editor: Matthew M. Vriends, Ph.D.

BARRON'S

First published in Great Britain in 1992 by
Frances Lincoln Limited, Apollo Works
5 Charlton Kings Road, London NW5 2SB

All inquiries should be addressed to:
Barron's Educational Series, Inc.
250 Wireless Boulevard
Hauppauge, NY 11788

Library of Congress Catalog Card No. 91-26712

International Standard Book No. 0-8120-4874-1

Library of Congress Cataloging-in-Publication Data
Piers, Helen.
    Taking care of your dog/Helen Piers: consulting editor, Matthew
M. Vriends.
        p.   cm. — (A Young pet owner's guide)
    "First published in Great Britain in 1992 by Frances Lincoln
Limited . . . London"—T.p. verso.
    Summary: A guide to buying, training, feeding, and taking care of
a puppy.
    ISBN 0-8120-4874-1
    1. Dogs—Juvenile literature. [1. Dogs.] I. Vriends. Matthew
M., 1937–   . II.Title.   III. Series: Piers, Helen. Young pet
owner's guide.
SF426.5.P54   1992   91-26712
636.7—dc20   CIP
                                          AC

Printed and bound in Hong Kong

2 3 4 5   9 8 7 6 5 4 3 2

Contents

Dogs as pets

A dog enjoys human company and affection, and becomes very attached to its owner and its family.

You could not choose a more intelligent and affectionate pet than a dog. Dogs were first domesticated over five thousand years ago, and they have lived as close companions to human beings ever since. A dog can be faithful and quick to learn obedience, which makes it easier to train than most animals.

Having a dog of your own is fun but the dog does need quite a lot of looking after in return. Every year hundreds of dogs are abandoned by people who buy them as puppies and then find they cannot cope with looking after them. So before adopting a puppy, it is important to think about what keeping a dog involves and to be quite sure you would be able to care for it properly and give it the kind of life it needs.

A dog is by nature a pack animal. If you adopt a dog, it will think of your family as its pack. You will be able to share the responsibility for your dog with your family, but if you are the one who feeds and trains it, you will be the leader of the pack.

These are some things you will want to think about before you adopt a puppy.

Would your dog get enough exercise?

If you do not live in the country, is there a park or open area where it is safe to let a dog off the lead to run about?

Could you afford to keep a dog?

Dog food is not cheap. Also your dog would need vaccinating once a year, and there could be other veterinarian's fees if it got ill.

Even when he is old and not able to run about so much, your dog still will depend on you and need your love and care.

Would you have the time?

You will need to feed your dog once a day (four times a day while a puppy), train it, and take it for walks.

Would your dog be left alone too much?

If everybody in your family is out at work or school all day, it would not be kind to keep a dog, unless you have two for company. A dog can be left for a few hours, but if it is alone all day it will get lonely and very unhappy.

What would you do when you went on vacation?

Would somebody look after the dog for you?

Dogs can be boarded at kennels, but it is expensive.

Is there an asthma-sufferer in the family?

If so, seek medical advice first. Allergies to dog hair may make the asthma worse.

The right dog for you

Dogs vary a lot in size, temperament, and how much exercise they need. Choosing the right kind of dog for you and your home will depend on whether you live in a town or the country, how much time you have to exercise and groom your dog, and how large and strong a dog you can handle.

A puppy or an adult?

If this is your first dog, it is best to get a puppy. Adopting a stray adult dog from an animal shelter would be doing it a great kindness, and it might turn out to be a faithful, well-trained dog. But it might not have been treated well in the past and have bad habits that are hard to break, in which case handling it would need skill and experience.

Male or female?

Both make equally good, affectionate pets, although male dogs tend to be more independent. But read page 28 before deciding which to have.

Dogs come in all shapes and sizes. If you live in a town, or if you want to train and handle your dog without a lot of help from an adult, you would do best to choose a small or medium-sized dog.

This little crossbreed is a very good size — small enough to carry, but robust and full of energy.

Pedigree, crossbred, or mongrel?

A *pedigree* or *purebred* dog is one whose ancestors were all of the same breed. A *crossbred* is one whose mother was of one breed and its father of another. A *mongrel's* ancestry is very mixed, and usually unknown.

Pedigree puppies are expensive to buy, but the advantage of getting a pedigree — or a crossbred, to some extent — is that you have a good idea of what it will be like when it is fully grown. It is more difficult to tell how big a mixed-breed puppy will grow, if it will be easy to train, noisy or quiet, and whether or not it will be an energetic dog that needs a lot of exercise.

See the following pages for more about different breeds of dog.

Mongrels make just as good pets as pedigrees and many people prefer them. They tend to be hardier than many pedigree dogs, and they are cheaper to buy.

Another thing to consider is whether there are very young children in the family. Some dogs, like this Labrador, are more patient with little children than others.

Different breeds

Tibetan Terrier
Size: small/medium
Very healthy, affectionate, good companion. Needs daily brushing.

There are over a hundred different breeds of dog, so if you decide to buy a pedigree, it is a good idea to study a book that lists all the breeds, with photographs and details about their temperament, and how much exercise and grooming they need.

If you have friends who own a breed of dog you think would be right for you, ask them to tell you what it is like to look after.

Things to find out about a particular breed
How big do they grow?
How much exercise do they need?
If your home is in a town, do they adapt well to town life?
Do they need a lot of grooming?
Are they likely to be aggressive towards other dogs or towards strangers?
How easy are they to train?
Are they quiet, or do they bark a lot?

Dachshund
Size: small
Hound. Loyal, affectionate, sense of fun. Prone to back injury, so must not put on weight. Must be trained not to jump on and off furniture.

Scottish Terrier
Size: small
Intelligent, brave, good guard dog. Needs plenty of exercise and firm training. Only good with children if used to them as a puppy.

Many types of dog were originally bred to do some particular kind of work, and this still shows in their temperament.

Hounds (breeds used for hunting above ground) and *working dogs* (breeds trained to herd other animals) all need space to roam around in, so are best kept in the country.

Terriers (bred to hunt animals that burrow underground) and *gundogs*, like spaniels and retrievers (trained to bring back game birds shot down by their masters), need less exercise and are faithful and obedient. They are happy in a town if there is a park for them to run in.

Other breeds, like the Tibetan Terrier and the Cavalier King Charles Spaniel, have only been kept as pets and companions. These will adapt to living in most homes, either in the country or in a town. There are also *miniature* breeds. These are often too delicate to stand up to a lot of romping and rough play.

Beagle
Size: medium
Hound. Cheerful, very healthy, good with other pets. Needs careful training or will wander.

Labrador puppy
Size: medium
Gun dog. Affectionate, faithful, trustworthy. Needs enough exercise or puts on weight.

Cavalier King Charles Spaniel
Size: small
Good-natured, clean, cheerful, obedient.

Getting ready for the puppy

Checklist

You will need:
- dog bed
- blanket
- food dishes
- water bowl
- toys
- grooming kit
- old newspapers

You will *not* need a collar and lead until your puppy is three months old (see page 20).

Your new puppy will settle in more quickly if everything is ready and comfortable for it before you bring it home.

You cannot expect the puppy to be house-broken yet, so until it has learned to be clean, you will want to keep it in one room most of the time. Choose a room with a floor that is easy to wash if necessary, but warm, and near the family, so the puppy is not lonely.

The puppy will need a bed, a place of its own to retire to even in the daytime. This should be kept in a warm corner out of drafts, but not close to a boiler or radiator. Line the bed with newspaper for warmth, and a blanket or old sweater for the puppy to snuggle into. Remember, if you buy a bed to fit your puppy now it soon will be too small. A cardboard box will make a comfortable bed until you see how big your puppy grows.

Puppies chew anything they can get their teeth into, so make sure there is no electric wiring it could bite and get a shock from, or anything it might play with and hurt itself on.

If your puppy is going to play in the garden, make sure there is no way it could get out, especially onto a road. Are there any railings, a gate, or a hole in the fence it could squeeze through? If there is a pond, you may need to put wire netting around it temporarily.

Food dishes and water bowls may be stoneware, plastic or stainless steel.

The grooming kit should include a bristle brush for a short-haired dog or a two-sided wire/bristle brush and blunt-ended scissors for a long-haired. You will need a towel, a comb and a rubber grooming glove too.

A dog bed can be rigid plastic or a basket as shown. Bean bags and foam rubber beds are not good for puppies as they chew them.

The first step in housebreaking a puppy is to teach it to wet and dirty on newspaper. Make sure you have a good supply.

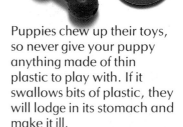

Puppies chew up their toys, so never give your puppy anything made of thin plastic to play with. If it swallows bits of plastic, they will lodge in its stomach and make it ill.

11

Buying a puppy

Pedigree puppies, like the Cavalier King Charles puppies shown here, can be bought directly from breeders, and from some pet shops. They are also advertised in dog magazines but make sure you see the puppies with their mother before buying.

Through friends you may hear of private owners with puppies for sale, or you can ask at your veterinarian's office or local animal shelters and animal protection societies if they know of any puppies needing homes.

It is quite common to choose a puppy when it is a few weeks old, and then to leave it with its mother until it is two to three months old.

Take time choosing your puppy. Remember, looks are not everything. A puppy that comes to you fearlessly and wants to play is a better choice than one that runs away and hides, however good-looking it is.

There are some important things to find out about the puppy you choose:

How old is it?
Between nine and eleven weeks is best. By then the puppy will be weaned and independent enough to leave its mother.

What food is it used to?
Also ask how much it is fed and how often. You should keep to the same diet at first.

Is it a healthy puppy?
A healthy puppy should be alert and ready to play. It should have clear, bright eyes, not bloodshot or runny. Its coat should be clean, without bare or sore patches. Its ears should be clean, without any waxy deposits inside. There should be no sign of diarrhea (dirt around the tail), or of fleas.

Has it been vaccinated?
If it has, you will be given a certificate. If not, have it vaccinated as soon as possible (see page 24).

Has it been treated for worms?
If not, consult your veterinarian about this.

Is it partly housebroken?

Pedigree certificate
If the puppy is a purebred, you should be given a certificate stating its date of birth and ancestry.

Remember
- How old is the puppy?
- What food is it used to, how much, and how often?
- Is it healthy?
- Has it been vaccinated?
- Has it been treated for worms?
- Is it partly housebroken?
- If a purebred, it should have a pedigree certificate.

If traveling by train or bus, you should take your puppy home in a carrying box or basket. Ask if you may have a piece of old bedding to put in it. It will help him feel more at home.

Taking the puppy home

Your puppy will feel more secure if you carry him in a blanket. It will encourage him to settle down, and he may even drop off to sleep.

If you travel home by car you will be able to carry your puppy in your arms.

Ask whoever is driving to go as smoothly as possible, for the puppy has probably never traveled in a car before, and too many jolts and sudden stops could make him feel sick.

On a long journey, you will need a drinking bowl and water, and some newspaper to put down in case the puppy wets. Never leave the puppy alone in the car if the weather is at all hot.

Don't forget that until your puppy has had his first course of vaccinations, it is not safe to let him walk in the street, where he might pick up an infection from other dogs.

When you get home, show the puppy his bed; give him something to eat and a drink of water; then let him explore the room quietly. Do not overtire him by playing with him too much. Puppies do need to sleep a lot. You can take him into the yard if the weather is fine, but for the first few days do not leave him out there alone. There may be dangers you have not anticipated.

Where is your puppy going to spend the night?

Decide right from the beginning whether your puppy — even when he is grown up — is going to sleep in your bedroom or on his own. Remember, once he gets used to spending the night in your room, it will be very difficult to break the habit.

Puppies often cry during the first night, because they miss their mother and the other puppies. Try not to go to your puppy every time he whimpers, though you can call some comforting words from the next room. After the first night or two, he will feel more confident and settle down without crying.

Be careful how you introduce the new puppy to other pets. An older cat or dog must be made a fuss of when first shown the puppy, so that it does not feel neglected. Never leave them alone together while the puppy is still small.

A puppy will be less lonely during the first nights in his new home if he has a warm hot water bottle in his bed and a quietly ticking clock. These will help him feel he still has the company of his littermates.

This kitten and puppy are both young, so they soon will make friends.

15

Housebreaking

Decide on a word to use when your puppy relieves himself. Always use the same word, and he soon will recognize it and know what you want.

When you replace the soiled newspaper, if you leave a small piece behind the smell will encourage him to come back and use it next time.

Puppies can be trained to be clean without too much difficulty, but you must be patient and not expect your puppy to understand at once. If he dirties in the wrong place he is not being naughty, because he does not know any better. Also, like a baby, he cannot yet control when he wets or dirties. So don't punish him. Only praise him when he uses the right place.

Start by teaching him to use newspaper spread out on the floor. Whenever he behaves as if he wants to relieve himself — he will probably whimper, turn in circles, and sniff the floor — lift him up quietly, take him to the newspaper, and hold him there gently until he has finished. Then praise and make a fuss over him.

If you have a yard, start to take your puppy out first thing in the morning and after his meals. These are the times he is most likely to want to do something. He probably will prefer using the backyard and begin to sniff at the door and bark when he needs to go out.

If your puppy makes a mess on the floor, wash the floor thoroughly and then rinse it with vinegar in the water. The vinegary smell will discourage him from using the same place again.

Most puppies are housebroken by the time they are six months old.

If you live in an apartment without a yard

It will take longer to housebreak your puppy if you have no yard, because you cannot take him outside until he has had his first course of vaccinations.

When your veterinarian says it is all right to walk your puppy in the street, begin to take him out at the same times as if you had a yard. At first you can place newspaper in the gutter to show him that it is the right place to use. Never let him use the sidewalk.

Dog feces contain germs which can cause people serious illness, so never let your dog mess on the grass in the park. Many parks have dog toilet areas which your dog can use before you let him loose to play.

You can buy special disposable trowels and plastic bags for removing your dog's messes.

If you have no yard, training your dog to use the gutter will take up more time, because you will have to walk him until he feels the need to relieve himself. To begin with, you may find it helps him to understand what is expected of him if you put a newspaper down and reward him with a piece of dog candy or a biscuit when he gets it right.

Feeding

For the first two weeks, feed your puppy the food he has been used to. After that you can try different foods to find out which he likes best.

Leave a bowl of fresh water down at all times.

Feeding your puppy

If you were not given advice on feeding when you bought your puppy, follow the diet sheet below. It is hard to say *how much* he will need, as size and appetites vary. Start by putting down a small amount — say, a saucerful at each meal. If he gobbles it all up at once and still seems hungry, he needs more.

If your puppy has diarrhea during the first few days, this could be caused by the stress of leaving his old home, and have nothing to do with feeding. Try giving him only well-cooked rice with boiled chicken or fish, and make sure he drinks plenty of water. If he is not better in two days, you should consult your vet.

Diet sheet for a growing puppy		
Age		
1–4 months	Early morning	Dry baby cereal mixed with a little milk.
	Midday	Chopped meat (beef, lamb, or chicken) or canned puppy food, both mixed with an equal amount of dog meal softened in gravy, water, or milk.
	4 pm	The same as midday feeding.
	6–7 pm	The same as early morning feeding.
4 months	Eliminate early morning feeding, and give midday feeding earlier.	
6 months	Eliminate last feeding and move 4 pm feeding to between 6 and 7pm.	
9 months	Begin to feed as an adult. Give all food at one meal, preferably in the evening, except in the case of very small dogs whose food should be divided between two meals, morning and evening.	

Feeding an adult dog

Dogs need a diet of meat, mixed with carbohydrates in the form of biscuits and meal, and small amounts of cooked vegetables, as available. The meat can be fresh or canned.

Any kind of fresh meat can be given, but chopped beef is the best. Heart and liver are good — but not too often. All should be cooked, and mixed with the same weight of dog meal. Bones should be removed.

You cannot do better than give a good brand of canned dog food. This should be mixed with an equal quantity of meal (mixer) unless it says on the label that this already has been added.

Fresh water should be within reach at all times.

Dog biscuits are very nutritious and full of vitamins, and a handful can be given daily.

Dogs and puppies need to gnaw bones to keep their teeth and gums healthy. Raw beef marrow bones are best. *Never* give chicken, lamb, or chop bones, because they splinter. You can buy rawhide bones for puppies and dogs to chew on.

Rough guide to how much food an adult dog needs each day				
Weight of dog	Under 10 lbs	10–30 lbs	30–51 lbs	Over 51 lbs
Fresh meat (before cooking)	about 4 oz	about 8 oz	about 12 oz	about 20 oz
Cans — 14 oz	1/3–1/2 can	1/2–1 can	1 1/2 cans	1 1/2–2 cans

To weigh a dog: First weigh yourself alone. Then, with the dog in your arms, weigh yourself again. The difference will be the weight of the dog.

Obedience training

A choke chain must be put on correctly or it will injure the dog. The end fastened to the lead must come around the *back* of the neck before passing through the slipping ring.

Training a dog takes time and patience, but to own a dog that walks obediently to heel, sits down, and stays there until told to move, and comes when called, is worth any amount of trouble.

Training will consist of teaching your puppy to respond to a few simple commands, but before beginning serious training, he will need to get used to walking on the lead.

Your puppy can begin to wear a collar at three months. It should not be too tight, but not so loose that it can slip over his head. After a few days, when he is used to the collar, attach the lead and walk him around the house or yard for a few minutes each day. He may not like it at first, and pull and tug. Be firm, but not rough. Persuade him to follow you by praising and coaxing him.

On the next page are four basic commands a dog should learn to obey (demonstrated by an adult Golden Retriever). You also can train him to retrieve and carry. Always throw the ball or stick away from the dog to avoid hurting him.

For the "stay" and "come" commands, a special long training lead is often used. For the "heel" training, you may find it necessary to use a choke chain instead of an ordinary collar. This sounds as if it might hurt the dog. It won't, *as long as you put it on correctly*.

If you need professional help, find out if there are dog-training classes in your area.

Walking to "heel"
Have the dog on your left, close behind you. The lead is in front of your body, and held in your right hand with your left hand halfway down, ready to restrain the dog. The lead should be slack. If the dog drags on it, pull him back and say "Heel!"

Training to "sit"
With the shortened lead in one hand, gently press down the dog's hindquarters with the other, palm flat, as you say "Sit." *Never* press on his back, except close to the tail, or you may hurt him. Hold the lead vertical, so his head remains up.

Training to "stay"
Now teach your dog to stay there until told to move. Face him, raise one hand, palm towards him, and say "Stay" as you move away a step or two. If he follows, say "No," and begin again. As he gets the idea you can move further away bit by bit.

Training to "come"
From a short distance face your dog, call "Come!" and pat your legs. Increase the distance as he understands what you want. When he arrives make a fuss over him. At this point, the reward of a biscuit or dog candy may be given.

Exercise out-of-doors

Quite apart from the enjoyment they get from going for runs, dogs cannot stay healthy if they do not get enough exercise. They also get bored if they do not get out enough.

There will be times when you do not feel like taking your dog for a run, or you would rather be doing something else. But watch how his tail wags when he sees his lead, and his ears prick up when you say "Walk," and it will seem worthwhile giving up half an hour of your time.

Dogs have a highly developed sense of smell. For them half the fun of a run is to explore, nose to the ground, following interesting scents, as if they are finding out all the latest news.

You can have fun exercising your dog. Some dogs like jumping, others enjoy retrieving a ball, stick, or Frisbee.

It is not good – and in some places it is illegal – to let your dog roam alone and risk being run over or lost. But he might get out of the house without your knowing. So make sure he has his identification tag on his collar.

If at any time your dog slips his collar or you let go of his lead by accident, do *not* chase after him. He will think you are playing and run away from you. Call him and run in the opposite direction – then *he* will chase *you*.

The law and dogs

By law, the owner is responsible for a dog's behavior out of doors, and may be prosecuted if it fouls the pavement, causes an accident, attacks people or other animals, or chases farm animals. It is advisable to take out insurance against damage which could be caused by your dog.

Remember

- Keep your dog on the lead in the streets of a town, and in the country where sheep are grazing if he shows any sign of chasing them.
- Train him to sit while you wait to cross the road.
- He must wear an identification tag with your name and address engraved on it.
- Don't let your dog foul the sidewalk or the grass in the park.

These dogs have followed the scent of a rabbit to its burrow. A country dog has more freedom to roam at will, but must be trained never to chase sheep.

Health care

Vaccination is given by injection. Apart from a moment's discomfort your dog should not feel ill afterwards, though he may not eat for a day to two.

Your veterinarian will give you a certificate to prove your dog has been vaccinated, and remind you of the date the next injection is due.

Dogs generally have good health, but there are a few things you can do to keep them healthy and in really good condition.

Vaccination

Some diseases passed from one dog to another can be serious—even fatal. You must protect your dog against the more common infectious diseases by vaccination. The vaccinations most often given are for *canine distemper, rabies, infectious hepatitis, leptospirosis, kennel cough,* and *parvovirus.* A puppy must be vaccinated at six to eight weeks, again at twelve to fourteen weeks or as the vet advises, and after that once a year for the whole of his life — not just for his own sake, but because he could pass on disease to other dogs.

Treatment for worms

Worms are little parasites that can live in a dog's intestines. The veterinarian will give you powders or tablets to keep your dog free from them. You may need to repeat the treatment every six months. Treat puppies for worms at four weeks, and again at eight weeks.

Fleas

Inspect your dog regularly, even if you don't think he has fleas. The veterinarian or pet store can provide a flea collar, or one spray or powder to use on the dog and another for its bedding.

Grooming

Grooming not only keeps a dog's coat in good condition and gets rid of loose hairs, it massages his skin, and gives the dog a feeling of well-being.

Long-haired dogs need daily care. Use a wire brush first to separate the hair, but be careful not to scratch the dog's skin. Then comb the whole coat well, teasing out tangles. Finish with a bristle brush. Always brush and comb the way the hair grows. Matted hair can be cut away with blunt-ended scissors.

Short-haired dogs only need a weekly brushing with a bristle brush, followed by a stroke-down with a rubber grooming glove to remove loose hairs.

When you groom your dog, check that his ears are clean inside, his claws not split or growing too long, and that there are no bare patches in his coat. All these would need treatment.

Generally a dog does not need bathing more than three or four times a year, but if your dog is getting smelly, or is light colored, more often will do no harm. Try to get your dog dry as quickly as possible after he comes out of the bath.

Illness

Signs of illness

- diarrhea
- loss of appetite
- runny eyes
- dull coat
- general dullness and lack of interest in things
- teeth chattering and foaming at mouth. (This may be a fit. Keep the dog quiet and warm, and call in your veterinarian at once.)

Dogs can suffer from *heat exhaustion*. They cannot sweat to cool down, but only pant. This Shetland Sheepdog has found shelter under a bench on a hot day.

Never leave your dog in a car in hot weather, even with the windows open.

However well looked after, dogs do get ill sometimes — just as people do. If your dog seems unwell, is off his food, or has diarrhea for more than a few days, *don't put off taking him to the veterinarian.*

Do not try treating your dog yourself, and never give him medicines meant for people, unless your veterinarian definitely advises it.

It is a good idea to find a local veterinarian's address, telephone number, and office hours as soon as you get your puppy. Do not wait for something to go wrong first. It also is possible to take out pet insurance to help pay the veterinarian's fees.

Serious illness

Dogs can live to be between ten and fourteen years old, but accidents happen and some illnesses are unavoidable. It might happen that one day your dog is seriously ill, or has an accident, and the veterinarian advises that it would be kinder to put him to sleep — that is, give him an injection which would cause him to die without pain.

It will be very sad for you to lose your dog like this, but trust your veterinarian. He will know if nothing can be done to cure a dog, and if an animal is suffering it is kinder to put it out of its pain peacefully.

How to administer medicines

To give liquid medicine it is easier to use a syringe rather than a spoon. You will need somebody to help you. If they hold the dog's muzzle closed and a little raised, you can then squirt the medicine into the pouch of loose skin at the side of the mouth. Give the dog time to swallow before you release it.

To give a tablet, one person holds the jaws apart and the other places the tablet on the back of the dog's tongue. Then the mouth is held shut and the throat stroked to help the tablet go down.

Even a dog that seems quite fit should be taken to the veterinarian once a year for a thorough check-up and annual booster vaccination.

Mating

A dog can tell when a bitch is in season and may wander a long way to find her, perhaps staying away for several days, waiting outside her home for a chance to mate with her.

It is a natural instinct for dogs to want to mate, as it is for any animal. But it can cause problems with pet dogs, and many people have their dogs *neutered*. Neutering involves a simple operation, after which a dog cannot parent puppies, and has no desire to mate.

The main reason for neutering dogs is to avoid too many unwanted puppies being born. Sadly, at the present time, thousands of unwanted puppies are born each year.

The problem with keeping an unneutered male (dog) is that, if allowed out, it will wander looking for a mate, and risk being lost or run over. And if restrained from mating, it will be restless and may become bad-tempered.

A dog is first able to mate at about eight to twelve months. It can be neutered at any age.

Neutering a female dog (bitch) is called *spaying*. An unspayed bitch will not wander, but she will come into season (the time when she can become pregnant) twice a year from the age of around eight months on. At these times she must be kept in, or on the lead, for three weeks, or she will mate and have puppies, perhaps with an unsuitable dog. She also will bleed a little at these times, so she might have to be confined to one room.

A bitch can be spayed at any age, but the best time is before her first season — between seven months and one year. Ask your veterinarian to advise you about this.

If your bitch is not spayed, she might one day manage to escape, mate, and become pregnant. If you do not want her to have puppies, you can take her to the veterinarian within *two days* of mating and he will give her an injection to prevent her getting pregnant. Never try to separate dogs during mating. This can harm them.

Mating a purebred

If you want your purebred bitch to have pedigree puppies, you will need to find her a mate of the same breed. Dogs suitable for breeding are advertised in dog magazines, or you can write to her breed club (see page 31).

It will be fun for you if your dog has puppies, but they do make quite a lot of work, and you will find that you need help from an adult.

Birth and new puppies

You can make your dog a special box to have her puppies in. The sides should be high enough to prevent the puppies from tumbling out. The guard rail inside is to prevent her from accidentally lying on one of her puppies.

If your bitch is having puppies, it is advisable to find a book that gives detailed advice about the birth and rearing of puppies.

It also is important to take her to the veterinarian before or when she is first pregnant, and then again just before the puppies are due, to check she is well, and whether there are likely to be any problems.

For the first four weeks she will eat as usual, but later, as the puppies grow inside her, she will need three times as much food, including milk and a mineral/vitamin supplement.

Dogs usually give birth easily, and she will probably not need help having her puppies, although she will want somebody to stay with her quietly to reassure her.

Watch her carefully for the first week after the birth to make sure she shows no signs of illness. At about three weeks, ask the veterinarian to examine her and the puppies.

You will enjoy watching the puppies grow. For the first four weeks they will need only their mother's milk, but after that you can begin to wean them on to solid foods.

Useful information

Length of pregnancy	9 weeks
Number of puppies in litter:	
small breeds	1–6 puppies
large breeds	5–12 puppies
Puppies' eyes open at	10 days
Weaning can begin at	4 weeks
Puppies can leave mother at	8–10 weeks
Best age for a bitch to have her	
first puppies	1½ years
Life expectancy	10–18 years

Further reading

Communicating with Your Dog
Ted Baer, 1989
Barrons, Hauppage, New York, 1989

Complete Book of Dog Care
Ulrich Klever
Barrons, Hauppage, New York, 1989

First Aid for Your Dog
Fredric L. Frye
Barrons, Hauppage, New York, 1987

How to Teach Your Old Dog New Tricks
Ted Baer
Barrons, Hauppage, New York, 1991

Useful Addresses

American Kennel Club
51 Madison Avenue, New York, NY 10038

Canadian Kennel Club
2150 Bloor Street West, Toronto, Ontario M6 540

American Boarding Kennel Association
4574 Galley Road, Suite 400A, Colorado Springs,
Colorado 80915

Index